Books by Charlotte Brady

Och den fula ängelen föll

Villfarelser

Detaljernas tämjare

The Golden Passage Trilogy

As Silence Is Your Witness

Midnight Transit

The Last Star

Midnight Transit

MIDNIGHT TRANSIT

Poems

Charlotte Brady

ANTERIOR BOOKS

MIDNIGHT TRANSIT. Copyright © 2016 by Charlotte Brady. All rights reserved. This book, or parts thereof, may not be reproduced in any form without the express written permission of the publisher. Printed in the United States of America.

ISBN-13: 978-0-9976182-0-4
ISBN-10: 0997618205

Anterior Books
P.O. Box 832469
Miami, FL 33283
www.anterior.us

Cover design by Ingenious Tek Group

First Printing

In Transit

When the train stopped at the station, I got on.
My wagon was empty, broken seats,
luggage left behind. I sat down and waited—
dark outside the window, unfamiliar tracks.

No one can follow me from here on.

I'm waiting for dawn to come, waiting
for light to show the landscape.
I know it's coming. Apart from that
I know of nothing.

The train starts moving and I am on my way.
In the window, a tiny golden rim
kisses the surface of a lonely Earth.

Blind to Light

Searching for your face in darkness,
my hands move over a wall's surface.
I'm colorblind and blind to light.

Where is the love that makes everything
worthwhile? Where is the rest you offer
when I find you?

I have contaminated the world with darkness;
it's devoured by my shadow. It's because of me
there is death and suffering.

I go on searching for you while watching
countless lives die inside my heart.
I am a killer and a warlord—let me find you,
let me be love again.

Wide and Deep

I was called through darkness, my answer
was faint. I didn't speak the language.
Many times I didn't understand
it was a calling; I was afraid.

How can fear and longing be known as love?
A question I could not yet pronounce
and, therefore, it didn't beg an answer.

In the beginning, only darkness was.
In the beginning, only the call was,
it echoed wide and deep, I listened.

And I hated it with the same passion
I would later use for love.

Darkness

I want to go now
alone and naked
into the dark
I want to go.

I want to go now.
I'm not afraid
of the sunset
anymore.
I watch
the darkness
creeping in.

I want to go now.

The palm leaves
turn black
against the sky.
The sun melts
into the ocean.

I'm not afraid now.
I'm waiting
for the darkness
to settle in my heart.
Waiting for the
darkness.
Waiting, waiting
for its embrace.

Unremembered Love

I am only interested in the inexpressible,
in the silent truth that permeates your being.
I am only interested in your name
before conception.

Who is calling you by your first name?
What is that echo in your veins?
There is a constant calling for you,
a calling in a million different ways.
Something wants you, all of you.
The you of all dimensions,
all the yous of you in universe.

I am the universe in you.
Your heart beats in me.
I am your desire
for that unremembered love.

Moment of Truth

An enormous void releases its fragrance.
It catches me. I am one with it.

Light dense as matter, stronger than gravity.
A hidden life, pulsating in coagulated ore.

I can hardly breathe. Dark waves
affix this body to the ground.

Am I free or bound?

Trust or Die

Nothing can save you because you are not salvageable.

Nothing of this world can redeem you.
Not your body, not your ideas, not your possessions. Eternally naked,
subjected to your own mercy.

How did you end up like this?

Who is the one forsaken, yourself or God?
We all arrive there, sooner or later.
We all have a choice, to enter or not to enter.
There will be no helping hands at this point.

You walk alone. You learn to trust or die.
You learn to love or you are lost.
The price is nothing you can afford.
The gain is loss of what you are not.

Vultures

The vultures in dark circles waiting for death.
Defeat is slow and vultures patient.
Their macroscopic eyes drive through matter
as they softly glide through the sky.

Who are they waiting for?
What in me are they chasing?
The wind loops offer no protection.
It's time to see.

Cosmic Wound

I am but a wound,
crimson blister, raw pulp
vibrating, bleeding hot,
as if all I am: a broken heart.

I am pain; big, dark, hollow.
What is the purpose
of this desert walk?
Why am I here?
Why is every breath
a thorn piercing my throat?
Why is every moment
reminding me of death?

I expand into a cosmic wound,
explosive progress, obliteration.
I am sucked in, consumed,
identified, slayed, remade,
negated—and still—
so sacredly alive.

Ugly Heart

With one foot in paradise and one in hell
I am free to choose but I don't.

Why can't I withdraw my foot from fire?
Why do I keep going toward my destruction?

I pray to be saved but nothing happens.
The world grows bigger and more
impossible each day.

Seduced, repelled, I stagger inside a shadow larger
than my frame. My heart must be ugly
if this world is a reflection of its dreams.

Through the Centuries

Traveling alone, I meet a friend.
I travel light but my friend travels lighter.
He puts something in my eyes
and I see the world differently.

Never cared much for travels
but this kind I like.

He talks of music beyond words.
He talks of mountains, paths
and abandoned children.
He paints the world.

In different centuries we walk,
When everything became silent,
I was prepared because of him.

Breathing Silence

At the bottom of the lake,
silence is breathing.
Nothing is beautiful.
Behind the mirror is complete
emptiness.
Nothing is freedom.
The world is breaking softly.
Nothing is everything.

Nothing is love, nothing is awake.
A bridge over the words—
I am nowhere to be found.

Consumed by immortality,
lost inside everything.
The breathing goes on, alone.

Die into My Love

How much love can I stand before I break?
—You were meant to break.

How can I assemble my shattered heart?
—Your heart was meant to shatter.

How much love can I bear without the means to share it?
—Love is meant to overflow.

But what if there are no takers?
—There are no takers.

Then I will burst.
—Then burst and die into my love.

Waves

Waves of love—impossible to curb.
Waves of now—impossible to limit.
All that is, is here.
The past is a mirage, the future never comes.
We are now, wrapped in love.
Close your eyes and look
for where the stars are hiding.
Look for that place
where you are welcomed as a god.

She Is Me

I'm carrying her body as if it were mine.
I comb her hair and brush her teeth.
I say her words and feel her feelings.
She is always with me.

I have a unique opportunity
to observe her life.
She shares the most intimate
details with me, thinking
there is only her.
She thinks we are the same.
Or rather she thinks I am her.

She doesn't realize yet
that she is me
and that we
are one.
She can't hear me yet,
my soft voice drowning
in her turmoil.

Catching Poems

Sometimes I pretend I'm a poet.
I start my poems from the end and
never expect myself to finish anything.
How could I when everything is a beginning?

My skin never belonged to me
and I sometimes miss my home.
I was always naked, as naked as a wind.

Now I'm catching poems in the bottomless
eyes of the forgotten empress.
It reminds me of who I once was,
who I am this moment.

Waves to Oceans

When the heart is soft, it absorbs the world's suffering. That's the way it was designed.

Painful steps lead to waves, waves to oceans.

Then the heart doesn't belong to you anymore.
It belongs to all.

It swells with emotion and beats in joy.
It returns to its original condition.

You say the name out loud—my friend!
You remember who you are.

Suffering melted, world transcended.
Heart still soft.

Devastating Beauty

Bring everything you have to me.
Show all your secrets,
your ugliness and your despair,
your devastating beauty.
They're all mine, too.
What you found in you—
everything you despised—
is also found in me.
Nothing is unfamiliar
as long as it is named.
Don't be ashamed.
Denial is unbearable.
You may not know it yet.
One day you will,
and you will shine
where only darkness
was before.

Soft Hearts Don't Break

Your heart absorbed the suffering,
and you noticed that it didn't burst.

It made you grow wilder for God—
deeper, more passionate. It made you brave.

It made your heart milder, more loving—
punctured by rapture, massaged by grace.

It made your heart tender as falling tears
It made your heart so soft, so liquid—
now it can never break.

Fist or Gentle Touch

The intimacy of my heart is fierce.
My face is open to receive a fist
or a gentle touch.
Aggression is brief and ugly.
It disappears immediately
into the ocean of my love.

I am fearless in connection
and expression.
I can take your hate.

I know where I'm going.
Love is showing me the way.
Even if I have to walk alone,
this is where I am.

The Works

All the butterflies I let loose,
you didn't notice them?
Your friend the little bird
and all the other animals,
they were sent especially for you.

Didn't you see the stars I lit,
the moon that followed
your every turn?

The twin birds this morning,
didn't you feel their adoration?
All things lost that reappeared?
The surprise, your unexpected luck?

Just look and you will see
how loved you are,
how constantly adored.

Journeys

I don't know anything of others' journeys.
I don't know where they change trains,
where they need to take a different turn,
where they say good bye, or reunite with
friends.

"Travel safe," is all I say when I meet them.
"Travel safe, I hope you find your destination."
We look at each other and then continue.

The light from my travel lamp is faint.
It doesn't reach very far, but I know
where to put my feet.

I see the edges of the road—a few bumps
ahead, loose gravel. It's late and I'm hungry.
I smell food and my feet are tired.

I think they are already there, I think
they have arrived. Their voices
like a whirlwind in the dark.

Learning a New Language

You have no grammar and no words
but your language can still be known.
I live by your holy syntax,
wrenching meaning out of emptiness.

You had love translated into life
and my life translated into being.
I opened my mouth and spoke.
I didn't recognize my voice.

You speak where oceans meet
and dictate my fragmentary tale.
You whisper the desire
I learned by heart at birth
but had to struggle to pronounce.
You are my dictionary,
my rule and my exception.

I am a full stop after a story told,
both insignificant and absolute.

Seedless

My friend, we are not different.
I borrowed your heart for days
and mine beat in someone else.
You can't remember
that I exist anymore and some days
I'm not so sure myself.

My heart is moving under my feet.
My hands are burning. I can't touch you.
You became a bird because
I couldn't feed you who I am.

I am tasteless, I go with everything.
You wanted sweet but I am seedless.

Counting

Brimming with emptiness
we can count only to one.
One sky. One Earth. One breath.
One heart. One mind.
Then everything stops.
"Why, why?" we cry while
tattooing the question mark
into our paper-thin skin.
As if to make us remember
not to ask more questions
(but we always forget)
as if to blind ourselves
to our despair and force
ourselves to count to a million—
without ever finding
the exact number
that describes our heart.

Ashes Gone

Surrender to what is: This is.
Is, do with me what you want.
Nothing perhaps.
Let me be a leaf,
a single thought.
Let me be a heartbeat,
a tiny raindrop.

Look, I am nothing now!
I am flying, I am everywhere.
There is nothing left to burn.

Ashes gone, milestones empty.
I am yours now.
I am your responsibility.

Unwritten Poem

Each day is like it was my first.
I am an unwritten poem, still unfolded.

What will happen today?
In what direction will my life flow?
I don't know. I cannot tell.
Anything can happen.

I go where the wind blows,
even if it's nowhere.

Liquid Gold

After the rain, sunshine translates water
into liquid gold. It's dripping
from the trees to the plants beneath.

Big leaves glow with thick layers
of golden water. I drink it with my presence.
I share it with the universe, let it circulate.

How sweet this reunion. I hope our nearing
to each other never ends.

The Grand Designer

Between birth and death
our story spans. Between
a predictable beginning
and a predictable end,
we are embroidered.

The color and quality
of the thread, material
and needle—it all differs.
The type of stitches,
the intensity of the work.

The grand designer
may be invisible
but it's his dream
we are creating.

The Roses

I stopped and smelled the roses.
I watched them whither and decay.
I allowed the sky to descend
and saw the Earth become my Mother.

I felt the thorns perforate my skin.
and watched the roses bud again.
I guessed their natural color.

I returned to the source of scent.
I watched it reveal its secret.
I made the sky descend
and I became a Mother.

I reset myself and saw the sky
within the rose, the Mother within
the sky, the thorn—as one.

Divine Puzzle

You show me the hooks on all the words
and how to connect them in the order you have
decided—a divine puzzle, my delight.

I follow you to the end—that's where you dip
my tongue in sweetness until it burns.

You open my heart by blowing gently inside it.
You dilate my pupils and make my hands
sensitive to touch.

I feel the sculpture that the artist chiseled,
it's as real as I am now, and centuries ago.

I Am It

Singing like a leaf,
burning like a sunset,
knowing like a bird,
rejoicing like a lizard,
trailing like a snail,
achieving like an ant,
loving like a rock,
sharing like a wind,
dissolving like a mist—

I am it.

Everything I watch I am.
It has my color, my essence—

I am it.

Stripped of qualities
mirrored by existence—
I am it, I am it.

Conversation with a Heart

You think I'm talking to you
but I'm talking to your heart.
You tell me what you do
but I want to hear about your being.

You dress yourself in your activities
and I admire you—you look spectacular.
You think your form is covering
your mistakes, but I only see your heart.

The Godless Mirror

If the mirror makes you look ugly, throw it out.
You are not meant to be reflected in a nasty way.
You are glowing around the edges.
You are the source of all.

Crack the mirror if it is distorted.
You know it is when you don't
recognize yourself. Heart pounding,
cracking rib cage open.

A little bird flew out, she was my friend.
When she died there was a sound of wings,
a few feathers on the ground.

This bird brought seeds from other worlds.
You made them sprout by loving them.
Look in the mirror now and see
all the little pieces—finally a single whole.

The Cage

The bird loves the cage
because the sky is limitless
and wings are not.

You showed me my cage
and what it was made of.

Pecking through the shell,
I knew wings were not enough.

I wanted wings unmarked
by limitation, I wanted
to become the sky.

Travel Companion

Did you ever feel lonely or were there many
friends at your wooden door?

Did you travel to different places?
Were you important and loved?

Did you drink the wine or was it only a
metaphor? I use it, both as a metaphor
and for intoxication. Nothing holy
about that, just an earthly comedy.

I ask questions as we walk. Were you as clever
as the scholars think or were you nothing but
love—or both?

No one takes me seriously when I say I met you, or when I say you are my teacher, that you come to me each morning and teach me from the silence in your words.

It seems to me you were a traveler but at the same time very still. I am not a traveler, I already left and yet I always travel with you.

Writing Poetry

I am your poem, write me. Write
about how I love to visit your garden. Write
about the red bird nesting and the snake
coiling in the bushes. Write
about the three blackbirds. Pretend
you have never seen me before. Find
a metaphor for my love. Picture
my feet touching the ground,
my hands longing. Measure
my body's occupation of a certain space. Find
the forgotten corners of the garden. Count
the fruit growing there. Remember
their names. Express
how I lick your face, ripe with eternity. Tell
how you receive me and show
how I receive your grace.

Fractured Heart

I wish I could give what I have
and share what I am. I wish
there was someone to receive it.

What I want to give is all I ever got.
All I ever got I offer and yet I am always full.

The membranes of the seeds are ready
to give in with a little moisture, a little soil.

The sun comes after.

A fractured heart is the most intact.
A heart that isn't fractured is a stone.

You Belong to Love

Remember who you are—
when you walk, when you talk,
when you smile.

Remember your heart
is beautiful and worthy.

Your eyes are memories of
timelessness and love.

Remember that darkness is just
forgetfulness, a lapse in time.

Pain and tears appear as soon
as you forget your brilliance.

Remember who you are.
Remember you belong to love
and love belongs to you.

Last Night

Last night I closed your closet door
so you wouldn't get sucked out into the universe—

as if we weren't already sucked out,
expelled and processed,

as if we weren't already fused into a body,
as if we weren't coming from nowhere,
going to nowhere and also resting in nowhere,

as if our fear had to do with the universe,
as if we weren't already here, beyond.

A Dream Come True

I know you dream of me.
Other dreams are not possible to have.
I am the dreaming and the dream,
your dream come true
and my own fulfillment.
We don't know each other.
Yet we've always known.

Popping Bubbles

Every thought pops like a bubble
when it collides with the essence
of what I am, of what who is.

Remnants of sparkly fizzle
fall to the ground and someone—
something, nothing—
grows deeper into infinity,
beyond blood, beyond tears,
beyond this.

Moon Poem

You know my poetry
before it's written.

You read between the lines,
and embroider my words
with a clarity I don't have.

You tie it all together
into a snake of silk.

You already know it's
neither silk nor snake,
neither dark nor light.

My poem is like the moon.
It's shining because of you.

Falling into the Pond

You won't hear what I say unless
you listen with your roots and see me
through the tiny bud inside your heart.

You won't recognize me unless
you have the courage to ask about yourself.

Some of me falls closer
to the source than usual.

Some of me falls into the pond,
makes rings.

Now you remember—I see you counting.
I know that look—you are falling into me.

Dreaming a Fig

I put a fig in my mouth as I'm dreaming of it.
It bursts and releases flavor over my tongue.

I dream the fig and eat it, too.
I dream I love you and love you, too.

Held captured in a body, we have no idea
how dangerous it is to be alive,
how threatened we are by our imagination.

The Grand Illusion

Tired of breathing
life into this dream.
Tired of watching it inflate,
deflate, inflate, deflate.
Tired of illuminating
the grand illusion.

Lovers and Seers

The wine is finished. Ruby red, it filled
my glass and I drank it. A world grew out
of me, inconsistent and mysterious.

My body was desire, my will its weapon.

The desires glittered in the night. Fake stars,
it was for me to pick and choose. I believed
and suffered. I had no friends nor enemies.

I had lovers, as I myself was a lover, albeit bitter.
I had seers, as I myself was a seer, albeit blind.

My lovers traced my body back to its origin.
I learned of pleasure.

My seers traced my heart back to its origin.
I learned of freedom.

I learned that pleasure ends but freedom doesn't.

Earthly Dreams

I hold you lightly until you want to fly.
My hands are open and your heart
transforms incessantly.
Yesterday it was a bird,
today it is a tree, tomorrow
a cascading stream.

I am the sun. I am the void.
I am the mouth that kisses,
the hand that holds,
the thought that embraces
everything you are.

We can stay or walk away.
We can meet or fall apart.
We can be divided or allow
ourselves to fall together,
to recognize each other
inside our earthly dreams.

May Love Blossom

May love blossom in hollow hearts
and heal the wounded souls.
The missing ingredient is always love.
Feel it in you first, then share.
Always write it on your list,
write it at the top and do it now.
Feel it in your toes, it's there.
Feel it in your hands, your throat,
your tongue. Love is now
and never later.

Sham

Let's pretend to be friends.
Let's pretend our souls
are not locked in embrace.
Let's pretend we don't know.
Let's pretend the depth
in our hearts is empty space.
Let's pretend we are not perfect.
Let's pretend the words
we say have meaning.
Let's pretend our silence
isn't love.

Always Now

Silence, stillness. Everything stops.
Peace deeper than darkness.
No talking, forgetting to think.
Alive is enough, alive is a love.

From here, right or wrong
is illusion and imprisonment.
From here, what is, is.
Always, now.

Rerouting

Every avenue is closed except the one
running through my heart.

Abandoned houses, empty roads.
Everyone is hiding in this neighborhood.

Life is getting smaller and smaller, yet
infinitely large on the other side of town.

I entered existence through the back door
and now I explore what it means to be alive.

Any road I choose leads to where I am,
no matter what I do to find a different route.

A Thing of Beauty

Questions, memories and meaning—
all those roads proved dead ends.

This is the final dead end, the grand opening.

You turn away and start over until there is
no more turning away and no way to start over.

You look up and see your face drawn across
the sky.

You look up and see your face as you begin
to know that disillusion is a thing of beauty.

Mad Pretention

I can take no credit for what I was offered.
I only discovered what was in front of me.

Perhaps I am pretentious but if I am—
can't you see beyond?

Perhaps I offended someone's sense
of hopelessness, but water drops on flowers
are too lovely not to mention and
the color drives me mad.

This Holy Moment

Oh, how everything starts anew.

You are born to yourself every second.
Your heart is the meaning of the universe.
Your heart is where everything begins.
It begins now. And now. And now.
Your rebirth in every moment is holy.
You are holy in this moment.
And this. And this.

Oh, how everything starts anew.

A Breath Wide

Life gave me certain humans;
you are my beloved.

Even when you hate me, you are my beloved.
Even when you attack me, you are my beloved.

Even though you don't know who I am,
I adore your concept of me.

Even though you don't know who you are,
I adore your heart.

Even when you don't know where you are going,
I adore your feet.

When you cry in loneliness, I hold you.
When you suffer, I am aware.

Life is only a breath wide. Let's love. Let's make each other's freedom present in our core.

A Cure for Longing

The sun drowned slowly in your eyes.
I didn't save it, I watched it drown.

The ocean was older than our hearts but
of the same material. The seagulls knew
our history and wrote it with their wings.

We lost count of heartbeats long ago, and now
timelessness must cure our longing.

In the distance, the cuckoo is disoriented again.
He knows there is no cure for longing
except love and yet more love.

The Lily Happens

The giant lily outside my window
opens for no reason and gradually
reveals itself to the sun.

It doesn't care who is watching
or not watching. It doesn't care
how long it takes. It doesn't care
if it's beautiful or not.

The lily happens.

Even when there is war and hatred,
it opens to the sky. Even when there is pain
and suffering, the lily goes into bloom.

Even when there is abundance and joy,
the lily continues to blossom.

It is, it ever is.

Digestion

Life expresses itself through me.
I should not interfere with dreams.

I am the lily opening, I am the cloud.
I am a kind word, the softest kiss.
I am also hatred, violence and death.

They express themselves as life,
like me. This is the hardest to digest.

Enter into the Moon

I have to enter into my aloneness.
I have to leave everything I have
at the gate. I have to stop running
after the moon's reflection and enter
into the moon itself. We are one.
I am the moon and its reflection too.

The longing is just at the border
of aloneness. One more step
and the longing is gone.
One more step and the aloneness is.
Stay at the door and the longing is forever.

If you try to embrace the moon's
reflection after drinking wine,
you will get a headache if you're lucky,
or drown if you are not so lucky.
The wine is kind and loving.
The moon is cool and distant.
Or so it seems.

Laughing with God

Parts of the journey you had to drag me.
I couldn't walk, my legs were paralyzed.

Parts of the journey you had to carry me.
I was too tired, too weak, too weary.

I couldn't even breathe without your help.

I went from dust to dust, from love to love.
I remembered your inscription, my fate.

Now I need to relax for the rest of my life—
don't make me laugh now, my belly hurts!

Blindly into Fire

An echo of myself, I still desire
what I once desired somewhere
in another universe.

The love I always knew
is with me but I have released it
from the objects and set it free.

I have closed my books
and began to read.
I have bathed in trust
and walked blindly into fire.

I think I'm getting ready
for my late arrival.

Listen to the Love

Listen to me as you listen
to a flower, with your mind
at rest and an open heart.

Listen to the vibrant colors,
the stages we are subjected to:
a seed that sprouts into a bud,
full flower, withering, decay.

Listen to the love
that infiltrates our growth.
Listen to how I look into your heart.
How I effortlessly reach
into parts you didn't know.

Traveling

Arrived at my destination.
I went on a journey
to reach my destination.

It was long and arduous.
I read the maps,
checked the compass.

South, North, East, West—

I tried every direction
even though I knew
I was already home.

Crazy Journey

I was called a long time ago,
but I didn't know how to answer.
I started walking, erratically and fast.
But wherever I went, the starting point
seemed to follow.

I moved, the starting point moved.
I stopped, the starting point stopped.

If I tried to retrace my steps,
the beginning proved elusive.
There was no way of turning back.

The sun descended, everything inside me
stopped. There was some sort of light,
not what I expected.

I recognized I was already at the center, always had been. I could not have known had I never made that crazy journey.

Nothing Happened

I took the road as far as it would take me.
It ended in a clearing suddenly,
and there was nothing more.

No more roads to take.
No more distant stations.
No more questions about directions.
No more complaints.
Even the eternal "what now?" dissolved.

The journey is over.
No more rails into the night.
It sounds like nothing
and it is; nothing happened.
Dawn broke and it was light.

Life of Death

I could never forget myself, so I found myself
staring into the eyes of death,
my constant companion; seductive, free.

Our attraction was mutual even though
we also resisted one another.
Our fights were bitter but always ended
in a burst of pleasure.

Death, my lover; youthful, passionate.
I surrender to you and give myself as I am.
You kissed me into life. I was reborn.
You left and I was found.

I Am What?

I am where I am.
Here.
I am what I am.
This.

Nothing is needed.
Nothing is missing.
Fallen out of a place
into the open
space.

The sun never sets
and a heart is reborn.
I am that I am—
home, that
sweet home.

The Crossing

I stopped by the end of my journey.
I sat down and enjoyed the beauty.
I knew I had almost arrived,
so there was no hurry.
Sand in my sandals,
tears in my eyes.

This is where I enter love, I thought,
this is where love enters me,
this is where you are waiting,
when I'm almost there.

Please know I'm helpless.
Please know I'm weary.
Not even the last steps
can I take myself.

I sat down and enjoyed the beauty.
There was no hurry anymore—
and so I knew I had arrived.

Becoming Water

And I became water on that day. Water with no source, no destiny and no direction; water living, being, twirling, playing in rays of light and darkness.

I have no name and no past, no purpose, future. I have freedom instead; freedom from the burden.

Life is flowing in that constant stream of nothingness. Obstructions gone, the merging with the ocean calmly taking place.

I Am the Search

Love lit my face and wiped out my memory.
Nothing is the same and nothing is different.

No more search because I am the search,
I am the question and the answer.

I'm ready to be built, to be demolished,
rebuilt and demolished once again.

The reunion wasn't what I thought.
It was here with me. It could not be sought.

The Very Beginning

Facing the abyss without breaking.
Seeing the face of death, kissing it.

This is where it ends, before you are sure
it even begins again.

This is where everything is strung together.

When all lights are gone you are illumined
by that which is not light, by that face

which has no death, only boundless life,
and an unknown name for love.

Acknowledgments

Thank you to my editor, Rosemi Mederos. Calm and composed, like a perfect sentence, she detects all my mistakes. She is indispensable in challenging me to be completely true to what I want to say. Thank you for making it possible for my poetry to meet the world.

And thank you *l i f e* for giving me, not necessarily what I want, but what I need, at any given moment.

Charlotte Brady has previously published two books of poems and a novel in Swedish. *Midnight Transit* is her second book in English and the second book in the trilogy, The Golden Passage. Her poetry explores the mystery of life and the search for freedom. After living in Sweden, New York, Jamaica, and Barbados, she has now settled in Miami where she lives with her family. Blending essential oils and making amazing fragrances is her favorite pastime.

www.charlottebrady.com

www.ingramcontent.com/pod-product-compliance
Lightning Source LLC
Chambersburg PA
CBHW050543300426
44113CB00012B/2236